Florida Wildlife
Coloring Book

Julie Burch

This book is dedicated to my husband, Larry, who opened my eyes to the natural world of Florida. The beauty and wonders of Florida's wildlife never cease to delight.

What if we take two of the most enjoyable and restorative parts of life, art and nature, and put them together? That's what we have here. This is an opportunity for you to get to know the natural world of Florida a little better while enjoying the pleasurable process of coloring. I love making art and teaching art, and I also love nature. The amazing diversity of wildlife living in Florida offers ongoing inspiration for all kinds of artists, and now, for you, in this coloring book. Take time to play, take time to enjoy nature, and don't forget to be creative and make art.

Julie Burch is a Florida nature lover and artist who has been making art all her life and teaching art for over twenty years to people of all ages. She is a certified Zentangle® teacher with a passion for pattern, ink, and color. Her master's degree is in Educational Curriculum, specializing in science and math. She lives in Florida.

She can be contacted at JulieBurch4Art@gmail.com.

The roseate spoonbill (*Platalea ajaja*) is a pink bird native to Florida and common along the coasts. They can grow to almost three feet tall. Great blue herons (*Ardea herodias*) are also common Florida shorebirds seen wading as they hunt fish and lizards. The tan-colored Florida panther (*Puma concolor coryi)* is the state mammal. The orange is the state fruit, and the bottlenose dolphin (*Tursiops truncatus*) is the state marine mammal. Florida was named after the Easter holiday, the Feast of the Flowers, by the Spanish explorer, Juan Ponce de Leon in 1513. Florida became a state on March 3, 1845.

The Zebra longwing (*Heliconius charithonia*) is the Florida state butterfly. It is found throughout the state and is common in the Everglades. It is especially fond of purple passionflower, where it prefers to lay its eggs.

The eastern gray squirrel (*Sciurus carolinensis*) is one of three species of squirrels living throughout Florida. This bushy-tailed member of the rodent family can grow up to 20 inches long. It gathers and hoards food for later use with amazing recall of where the food is hidden.

The great hammerhead shark (*Sphyrna mokarran*) enjoys shallow coastal waters and can also be found at depths of up to 300 feet. A 991-pound hammerhead was once caught off the Gulf coast of Florida.

Moon jellyfish (*Aurelia aurita*) are common in the waters around Florida. They are related to corals and have a nervous system but no brain. They often live in large groups in the sea. The moon jelly's sting is very mild and harmless to humans.

Loggerhead turtles (*Caretta caretta*) are the most common sea turtles in Florida. They can weigh 300 pounds. Their favorite place to nest is on Florida's sandy beaches.

Coral reefs are found off the southern shores of Florida and are home to a wide variety of marine life including colorful fish. Two bright examples are the blue tang (*Acanthurus coeruleus*) and queen angelfish (*Holacanthus ciliaris*).

The American river otter (*Lutra canadensis*) lives throughout Florida except for the Keys. They are social animals and are most active at night. A group is usually made up of a female and her offspring.

The sailfish (*Istiophorus platypterus*) is Florida's official saltwater fish. They can grow up to five feet long and over 100 pounds. The "sail" of the sailfish has lots of black spots.

The lined seahorse (*Hippocampus erectus*) can grow to seven inches long. It can be seen in shallow salt water clinging to sea grasses, coral, and mangrove roots. It has a curled tail, a horselike head, and a body covered with bony plates. It is the male who carries the babies in his pouch.

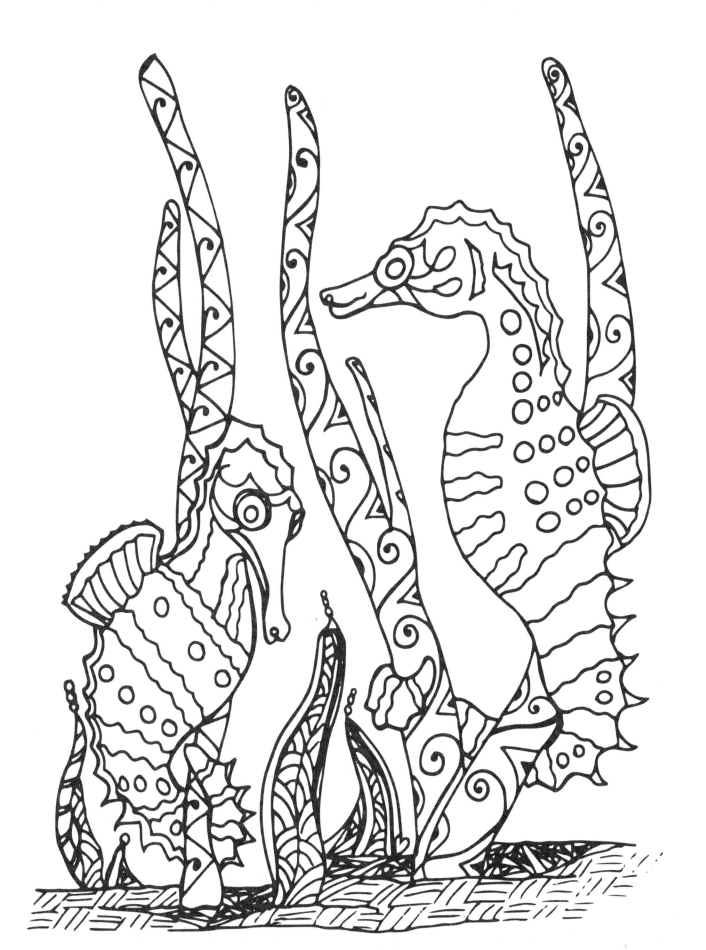

White-tailed deer (*Odocoileus virginianus*) can be found throughout Florida eating leaves, shoots, flowers, and, beware–landscaping. Their size depends on their habitat and ranges from 100 to 190 pounds. A subspecies, the Key deer, roams the Florida Keys and is smaller, weighing only 80 pounds and measuring about 27 inches tall.

The green anole (*Anolis carolinensis*) has the ability to change color from greens to browns in order to blend in with its environment. Sometimes called the American chameleon, it is not a true chameleon. The male has a pink flap of skin that hangs from his throat to attract females.

The northern cardinal (*Cardinalis cardinalis*) is common in Florida. A grain and seed eater, the male is bright red and the female is a duller reddish color. In this picture, they perch on a flowering bird of paradise plant (*Strelitzia reginae*), a colorful South African plant popular in Florida landscaping.

The playful bottlenose dolphin (*Tursiops truncatus*) is Florida's official saltwater mammal. They can be seen frolicking in bays and just offshore. These excellent problem solvers may be one of the world's most intelligent animals, second to humans.

The American flamingo (*Phoenicopterus ruber*) can sometimes be spotted in the Everglades, south Florida's "river of grass." When they hatch they are white. The pink color of flamingo feathers comes from their diet of algae and invertebrates. They travel to Florida from the Caribbean islands. There are very few remaining in Florida.

The American eel (*Anguilla rostrata*) dwells in both salt and fresh water along the east coast of North America. Its snakelike body can grow as long as five feet. Eels are highly adaptive and have the broadest diversity of habitats of any known fish species. These hardy fish have survived multiple ice ages. They go through distinct metamorphoses, each phase with a specific name: glass eel, yellow eel, silver eel. They are born in the Sargasso Sea area of the North Atlantic Ocean and migrate from there. Most make their way up inlets and into rivers, where they may live as long as 40 years. When it is time to spawn they return to the sea, lay their eggs, and then die. They hunt at night, eating fish, eggs, crabs, frogs, and whatever other animal matter they encounter in their habitat.

The anhinga (*Anhinga anhinga*) is a dark bird also called the snakebird or water turkey. They are most noticeable sitting at the edge of a pond with wings outstretched as they dry their feathers. They feed on the creatures of the pond, including small alligators and snakes. They prefer warm climates and slow-moving waters. The softshell water turtle (*Apalone ferox*) looks like a big leathery pancake, from one to two feet wide. They can be aggressive and bite. They prefer fresh muddy water and can tolerate brackish waters.

The nine-banded armadillo (*Dasypus novemcinctus*) has been a Florida resident since the 1920s and is now considered naturalized. This cat-sized mammal is covered with a bony armor divided by nine bands in the center. They have poor eyesight and dig in loose and sandy soil looking for grubs and plants to eat and may disrupt gardens and landscaping. They have long snouts and thin tails. The female produces one egg that splits into four identical quadruplets that are either all male or all female.

The black bear (*Ursus americanus*) is the only bear found in Florida. They weigh from 150 to 350 pounds. Their ears grow to adult length while young, giving a cub a large-eared appearance. Adult males have small rounded ears. They eat mostly plant foods supplemented with insects and animals, usually scavenged. They will eat almost anything and can smell food a mile away, which is typically the cause of encounters with humans. They enjoy eating acorns from the nine species of oak trees in Florida and feast on the heart and berries of palmettos. Females will den in palmettos in midwinter. They prefer woodlands and swamps where food is plentiful. They are excellent climbers, scampering up trees when frightened.

If you see a quickly moving long black snake in the yard it is likely a southern black racer (*Coluber constrictor priapus*). They inhabit a wide range of habitats both urban and rural throughout Florida. Nervous in disposition, they will flee to avoid contact. This snake is nonvenomous, although if cornered and frightened it will bite as a defense. Its diet is mostly lizards, eggs, birds, and frogs. It will smash them to the ground before devouring, so the constrictor classification is misleading. Its head is a smooth, scaly, narrow oval, and its tapered body can get up to 5 1/2 feet long.

The bobcat (*Lynx rufus*) is about twice the size of a house cat and has a short tail that appears "bobbed." The bobcat's ears are pointed, with little tufts of hair, and the body is tan with dark spots or bars. Bobcats sleep in little catnaps of two to three hours and so can be seen day or night, especially near the palmetto scrub areas they prefer for their dens and resting spots. They feed on small animals such as rabbits, squirrels, and birds.

Florida is home to many pelicans, both brown and white. The brown pelican (*Pelecanus occidentalis*) is the smallest of the eight species in the world: about 48 inches tall with about an 84-inch wingspan. Colonies of pelicans nest in mangrove areas along the coast. Skillful at fishing with their large bills, they can dive straight down and hit the water at high speed. They can also be found lingering around piers and docks waiting for fishermen coming in from a long day with extra bait; the pelican is happy to oblige.

The common buckeye butterfly (*Junonia coenia*) can be found throughout Florida. It is brownish-gray, with some orange, and with distinctive circular patterns, called eyespots, on its wings. The bright yellow Florida state wildflower, the coreopsis, sometimes called tickseed flower, is known to attract the buckeye. There are fifteen species of coreopsis in Florida. They are related to the daisy. Their peak blooming season is in spring and early summer, or in the fall.

The common octopus (*Octopus vulgaris*) is an intelligent invertebrate that is able to change colors to blend in with its environment. They hide from dolphins and sharks, who would find them a tasty meal. They can eject a cloud of black ink that allows them to swim away from predators. An octopus can even release and regrow an arm if necessary. They live about two years and can grow as long as four feet. They have been known to get into crab traps and crush and eat all the crabs.

The gray fox (*Urocyon cinereoargenteus*) is gray and white with some red in its coat. This doglike mammal grows to only about 13 pounds and has pointed ears and a fluffy tail. They prefer to live in wooded areas and are most common in northern Florida. Their diet is mostly mice and rabbits. This is one of the few members of the dog family that can climb a tree.

In a timeless Florida scene at the edge of a lake or pond, we see a heron wading among the cattails. The ibis hunts along the shore in the shadow of the state tree, the cabbage palm. Bass dart in the water and turtles sun on the bank. A noisy symphony of chirping, croaking, and whistling from countless unseen frogs, birds, and cicadas fills the air.

The largemouth bass (*Micropterus salmoides*) is Florida's official freshwater fish. This bass has a noticeable dip along its dorsal fin and the top jawline extends beyond its eye. They are a favorite fish for freshwater anglers and are plentiful in rivers and lakes throughout Florida. Adult bass eat smaller fish and insects, while the baby bass eat zooplankton (microscopic animals that drift in water).

The Florida panther (*Puma concolor coryi*) belongs to a group of large cats in the puma family that may also be called cougars or mountain lions. They purr, hiss, snarl, and growl, but they do not roar. Today it is an endangered species with only about a hundred thought to be in the wild. They roam parts of south Florida inhabiting wetlands, forests, and palmetto scrub areas. Growing up to seven feet long, they are at the top of the food chain and feed on other mammals, especially deer and feral hogs. Habitat loss, disease, and car accidents continue to threaten these graceful animals. They were chosen the Florida state animal by a vote of students throughout the state.

The graceful sandhill crane (*Grus canadensis*) grows to a height of 47 inches with a 78-inch wingspan. Found throughout Florida, they are less common in the Panhandle area. They prefer freshwater marshy areas, pastures, and ponds. They are often seen in family groups walking along the roadside hunting in grassy areas. The sandhill's deep trumpeting call is created by the unique structure of its windpipe. They mate for life, and juveniles stay with the family group for nine or ten months. In flight cranes hold their necks out like geese, which helps distinguish them from herons, who tuck back their necks. It is a protected bird considered threatened in Florida.

The mockingbird (*Mimus polyglottos*), Florida's state bird, is known for its wide variety of songs, mimicking the sounds of other birds. This mostly gray bird is about ten inches long. It will defend its nest diligently and swoop down on or chase away perceived threats. It can be heard singing throughout the day and even through the moonlit night. The mockingbird is known for its intelligence. In some cases, it has been shown to recognize individual humans.

The gopher tortoise (*Gopherus polyphemus*) is a land turtle, about ten inches long that can live up to 60 years in the wild. They have shovel-like front limbs for digging long tunnels, from 15 to 47 feet, in sandy soil. As many as 300–400 other species make use of the tortoise den. For this reason, they are an important species and vital to the ecology of their nesting area. These turtles produce only a handful of eggs per year, which are often feasted on by other animals. They eat low-growing plants and berries. Except during breeding season, they are solitary, roaming around a four-acre territory.

The great blue heron (*Ardea herodias*) waits at the water's edge, on tall legs, with a long graceful neck, and sharp eyes looking for lizards, fish, frogs, or snakes. It can be found near salt or fresh water. Because of the diversity of its diet, it has a range from Florida to southern Alaska. The great blue heron keeps an eye out for the unattended bait bucket, where a quick snack is easy picking. This majestic bird can be over five feet tall with a six-foot wingspan.

Florida is home to 27 native frog species. The southern leopard frog (*Lithobates sphenocephalus*) lives in shallow water throughout Florida except for the Keys. This is a greenish-tan frog with obvious spots and is usually about three inches long. They breed after heavy rains. You can hear the male's breeding call that sounds like a squeaky balloon. Thousands of eggs will be laid attached to submerged sticks and hatch after one to two weeks. Tadpoles are one to two inches long. They move through their tadpole phase in 60-90 days. These frogs hide in the vegetation at the edge of the pond and swim away from predators.

The Florida manatee (*Trichechus manatus*) is the state marine mammal. It lives throughout Florida in both fresh and salt water. They can grow up to nine or ten feet long and weigh from 1000 to over 2000 pounds. Believe it or not, they do not have much insulating fat and so they migrate to their favorite warmer waters when the weather turns cool. They can hold their breath up to 20 minutes. These gentle giants are vegetarians and large ones can eat up to 100-150 pounds of marine greens a day, earning them the nickname "sea cow." The calves nurse under the mother's flipper, and the two communicate with squeaks and chirps. They are most threatened by red tide and boaters.

The monarch butterfly (*Danaus plexippus*) is known for its orange color. Females have heavier black veins, and males have a black spot on each wing. Adult monarchs feed on nectar from a variety of flowers, especially pentas. Monarchs lay their eggs on milkweed leaves, and after about four days the black and yellow caterpillars hatch and begin eating the milkweed. Each caterpillar forms a protective chrysalis that is green with yellow spots. Here the caterpillar completely dissolves and reconstitutes in a new form. After two weeks, the butterfly emerges, dries its wings and flies. Monarchs are famous for their long north-south migrations. In Florida we have a resident population that can be seen year-round. We also can see the migrating butterflies in spring and fall.

Shallow reefs and mud flats are home to sharks and rays, who feed on many of the same prey. The southern stingray (*Dasyatis americana*) is found in coastal waters and in sand and mud flats. It can grow up to 200 pounds and can be as large as six feet across. It has a venomous barb near the base of its tail, but it is not aggressive to humans. The butterfly ray (*Gymnura micrura*) has a shorter tail. This diamond-shaped ray is wider than it is long and has a grayish color with faint spots to help it blend in with the sandy bottom. Its tail does not have a spine and is considered of little danger to humans. The nurse shark (*Ginglymostoma cirratum*) can grow to nine feet. It gives birth to more than 20 pups at a time. The nurse shark is often seen motionless near the bottom of a reef or mangrove island. They eat shrimp, mollusks, and small fish. Nurse sharks are rarely involved in attacks on humans.

The opossum (*Didelphis virginiana*) is a cat-sized animal covered with a gray and white coat and is the only marsupial found in the United States. They have a little pink snout and a naked tail and ears. The mother carries her honeybee-sized newborns in a pouch where they nurse and grow for about 80 days. They can then be seen riding on their mother's back for another week or two before striking out on their own. They will raid garbage, pet food left outdoors, and gardens or other readily available food sources. They seek wooded areas with a water source and are skilled climbers.

The osprey (*Pandion haliaetus*) is a hawk, sometimes called a sea hawk, and is a member of the raptor family. The osprey soars over water, then dives in and catches live fish. It has a hooked bill, a brown back, and a white underbelly (which helps distinguish it from a bald eagle, which has a dark chest). The osprey is about two feet long, with a wingspan as wide as six feet. When in flight they sometimes have an M shape to their wings. Look for their stick nests atop poles in the blazing sun—never far from water.

Florida is home to the largest and smallest of owls: the great horned owl (*Bubo virginianus*) and the eastern screech owl (*Megascops asio*). Screech owls are active at night. By day they hide out in trees and blend in with the branches. They occur in three different colorings: gray, reddish, and brown. They have yellow eyes and are about eight inches long. They mate for life and are devoted to their mates, talking to one another and preening each other. This little owl is more often heard than seen. It produces an unmistakable purring trill. The great horned owl is common throughout North America and although nocturnal, can sometimes be spotted hunting at dusk. This largest of the owls has distinctive pointy tufts on its ears and eyes that glow yellow or orange. Its striped body and powerful hunting have earned it the nickname "tiger owl." The owls feed on small animals although the great horned owl will take a larger animal such as a rabbit. They have a distinctive call: hoo hoo-hoo hoo hoo.

Florida is home to both marsh rabbits (*Sylvilagus palustris*) and eastern cottontail rabbits (*Sylvilagus floridanus*). The marsh rabbit, which prefers to roam near water, is smaller, darker, and has shorter, rounder ears than the cottontail, giving it a guinea pig-like appearance. They have only a small tuft for a tail and are known to walk more than hop. The cottontail has distinctive long ears and a fluffy white tail that can be seen as it hops away.

The intelligent raccoon (*Procyon lotor*) is marked by a black mask around its eyes and a bushy tail. This dog-sized mammal roams the entire state of Florida, preferring to stay near water and use trees for shelter and climbing. They feed off fruit, garbage, eggs, and small animals. They are good hunters in the water, catching frogs and crayfish with their dexterous front paws. They weigh as much as 15 pounds. They are often found in urban areas, where they scavenge garbage and are often considered a nuisance.

Florida is a temporary home to many migratory birds. Some stay for the winter and others pass through on their journey farther south. The ring-necked duck (*Aythya collaris*) is a diving duck, plunging underwater to seek food. It prefers a sheltered pond, where it feeds on vegetation and insects. Unlike most diving ducks, it has the ability to take off directly from the water's surface without a running start. Despite its name, you can almost never see the ring on its neck. The mottled duck (*Anas fulvigula*) is a relative of the mallard, but with a duller mottled brown and tan appearance. It is a dabbling duck, meaning that it feeds by straining surface water instead of diving. It upends its body to reach below the surface. Mottled ducks may also feed as they walk along the water's edge.

Sandpipers are shorebirds that chase the waves along the beach feeding on small mollusks. The sanderling sandpiper (*Calidris alba*) is about eight inches long with a fluffy white underside and black legs. They can be seen in groups on sandy beaches in the winter. Breeding birds fly north to the high arctic tundra and return south when winter approaches. The herring gull (*Larus argentatus*) is a common seagull in North America. With its white head and gray body it represents what most people think of when they consider a seagull. They migrate north to breed in the summer, and many are lucky to spend their winters in sunny Florida. Although they prefer to drink fresh water, they have special glands near their eyes that secrete salt so that they can drink salt water.

The Florida horse conch (*Triplofusus giganteus*) is the state shell. This orangeish shell belongs to a sea snail, a soft-bodied invertebrate that can grow up to two feet. It is the largest gastropod in American waters. They are found in sand flats and coral reefs in shallow waters. It feeds on mollusks. Many species of starfish or sea stars are found in the waters around Florida. They are rough-bodied echinoderms with little tubelike feet. While it is exciting to see them in shallow sandy coastal waters, a fishing license is required to collect live specimens. The fiddler crab (many species of the genus *Uca*) lives in the sand near the water's edge and is a favorite food of fish, birds, and mammals that live near the shore. Fossilized sharks' teeth can sometimes be spotted among the seashells, especially in the Venice and Jacksonville areas.

A variety of woodpeckers call Florida home. Commonly seen are the pileated woodpecker (*Dryocopus pileatus*) and the red-bellied woodpecker (*Melanerpes carolinus*). The pileated woodpecker is a large bird, about as big as a crow, and is mostly black with white markings and a distinctive red crest creating a point atop its head. They produce a loud "kekeke" sound and pound very loudly on trees. The red-bellied woodpecker is a medium-sized bird with a noticeable black and white pattern down its back. It has a red cap that extends down the back of its head to the shoulders and a dusting of red on its white underside.

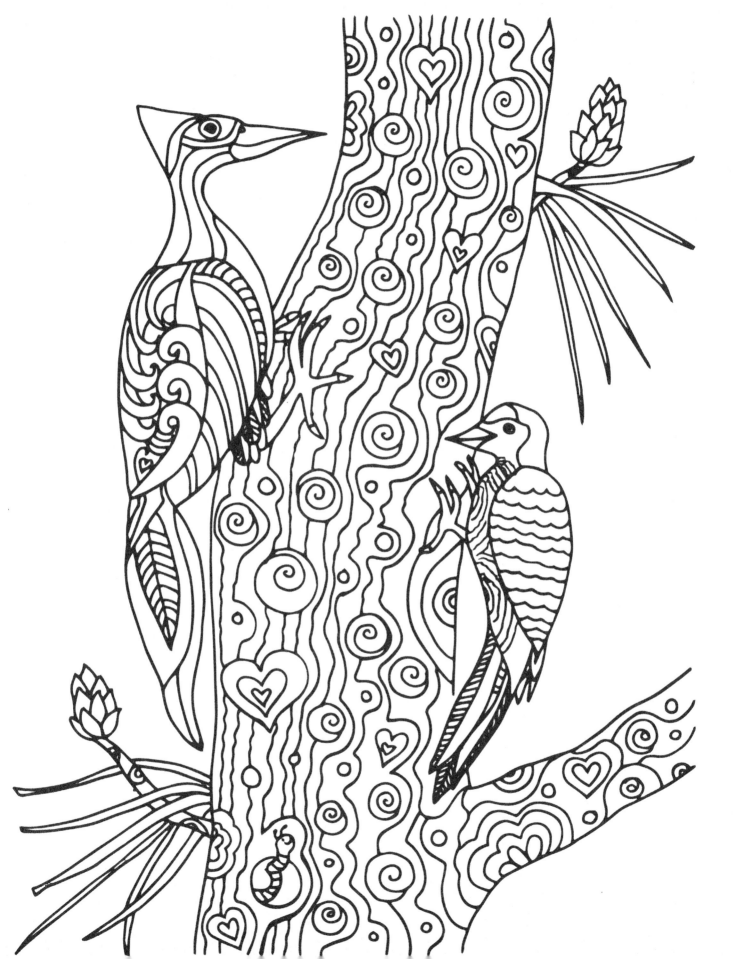

Florida alligators (*Alligator mississippiensis*) are protected reptiles that can grow to between 10 and 14 feet long and up to half a ton in weight. They will eat whatever is available, even young alligators. People should avoid them and never feed them since this could cause them to approach and endanger humans. Alligators prefer fresh water: ponds, lakes, and slow-moving rivers. They can be seen enjoying the sun on the river banks, where they warm themselves, preferring temperatures above 82°. A special structure of their eyes causes them to shine red. The broad snout of the alligator sets it apart from the V-shaped snout of the crocodile.

Online resources used in this book and to get more information:

fws.gov	(U.S. fish and wildlife service)
flmnh.ufl.edu	(Florida Museum of Natural History)
flawildflowers.org	(Wildflower information)
allaboutbirds.org	(The Cornell Lab of Ornithology)
myfwc.com	(The Florida Fish and Wildlife Commission)
animals.nationalgeographic.com	(National Geographic)
flseagrant.ifas.ufl.edu	(University of Florida IFAS Extension)
butterfliesandmoths.org	(Information about butterflies and moths)

For more books from Pineapple Press, visit our website at *www.pineapplepress.com*. There you can find author pages, discover new and upcoming books, and search our list for books that might interest you. Look for our weekly posts and giveaways, and be sure to sign up for our mailing list.

If you loved this book, look for these related books on our site:

Drawing Florida Wildlife
If you love watching Florida birds and other wildlife, searching for nests, and identifying trees and plants, here is a new way to enjoy it all—by learning to draw what you see. Whether you are embellishing field notes or just enjoying a new skill, you will appreciate the easy directions in this guide to drawing Florida's diverse wildlife and plants.

Florida's Birds
This illustrated guide to Florida's Birds includes full-color illustrations and detailed descriptions of each species, and covers such topics as exotic and endangered species; bird conservation and study; finding, attracting, and feeding birds, bird problems, and the care of sick and injured birds.

Exploring Wild South Florida
An insider's guide to the natural areas of south Florida, from Hobe Sound in the east and Punta Gorda in the west down to the Keys and the Dry Tortugas. Includes Everglades National Park, Big Cypress National Preserve, the coral reefs of both Biscayne National Park and Pennekamp State Park, and Ding Darling National Wildlife Refuge and Corkscrew Swamp, as well as many smaller state and county parks, recreation areas, and nature centers. Includes maps and information on camping, boating, hiking, fishing, tours, and more.

Our Sea Turtles
Blair and Dawn Witherington intimately reveal the lives of sea turtles in this award winning book. The book's pithy, well-organized sections are lavishly illustrated. It is a guide for anyone who is the least bit curious about these fascinating marine animals. Bite-sized installments harmonize with multiple images on each page to make this book a unique and entertaining resource. The story it tells covers understanding, experiencing, and saving Our Sea Turtles, with descriptions of how these endangered animals contribute to our happiness and why they deserve a helping hand.

Magnificent Florida series
Tour Florida's through these breathtaking photos of Florida's coasts, uplands, and wetlands by James Valentine, with scientific explanations by Bruce Means.

Paynes Prairie
This new paperback edition of *Paynes Prairie* still offers the sweeping history of the shallow-bowl basin in the middle of Florida, just south of Gainesville, but now adds a guide to outdoor activities that can be enjoyed in the state preserve there today, along with maps of trails for biking, hiking, and canoeing.

Those Amazing Animals series
These eighteen children's books present amazing animals in an entertaining way with large photos and amusing drawings. Each book includes information on height, distribution, kinds, speed, herds, endangerment, food, family structure, babies, and more.

Florida's Living Beaches
Florida has 1200 miles of coastline, almost 700 miles of which are sandy beaches. Exploring along those beaches offers encounters with myriads of plants, animals, minerals, and manmade objects—all are covered in this comprehensive guide with descriptive accounts of 822 items, 983 color images, and 431 maps. Beginning with the premise that beaches are themselves alive, this guide to the natural history of Florida beaches heralds the living things and metaphorical life near, on, and within the states sandy margins. It is organized into Beach Features, Beach Animals, Beach Plants, Beach Minerals, and Hand of Man. In addition to being an identification guide, the book reveals much of the wonder and mystery between dune and sea along Florida's long coastline.

Florida's Seashells
A visit to any Florida beach can spark curiosity about seashells. Satisfy questions about the names and lives of seashells by comparing beachcombing finds to color photographs representing hundreds of individual shells. This book heralds the diversity of Florida's seashells and presents them in the way they come to us on beaches. Florida's seashells offer both collectors an outlet for the appreciation of natures splendor. This guide includes species common to the southeastern United States and the Caribbean, with full color photographs and maps throughout. Guide organization is simple, and images show shells as they would be found on beaches, not in museums.

Flowering Trees of Florida
If you can't get enough of majestic trees, brightly colored flowers, and anything that grows from the ground up, you'll love this guide to 74 outstanding tropical flowering trees that will grow in Florida's subtropical climate. From the huge canopy of red blossoms on Royal Poinciana, to the eye-dazzling yellow of Tree of Gold, the most breathtaking of Florida's flowering trees are represented within the pages of this full-color book.

Myakka
Discover the story of the land of Myakka. This book takes you into shady hammocks of twisted oaks and up into aerial gardens, down the wild and scenic river, and across a variegated canvas of prairies, piney woods, and wetlandsall located in Myakka River State Park, the largest state park in Florida. Each adventure tells the story of a unique facet of this wilderness area and takes you into secret places it would take years to discover on your own.

The Biohistory of Florida
Florida has an amazing biohistory. Its fossil record reveals that 8-ton ground sloths, giant beavers, and tiny horses once roamed its 66,000 square miles. Its human history is the story of people who arrived some 12,000 years ago after a journey that took them from Asia across the Bering land bridge and then south across the North American continent. Today, Florida is home to historic St. Augustine, the futuristic Kennedy Space Center, and the mysterious Everglades. Hosting a diverse ecology and a rich human history, Florida now faces a tenuous future as its natural resources are depleted, new species of plants, animals and diseases invade, and climate changes loom. This fascinating biohistory, prehistoric to present-day, and with an eye to the future, is told with verve and clarity. The result is a fascinating story of how they all interrelate.

CPSIA information can be obtained
at www.ICGtesting.com
Printed in the USA
BVOW03s0908011116

466169BV00002B/7/P